The Fun Run

Practising phonemes of more than one
letter and simple polysyllabic words

First published in 2007 by
Franklin Watts
338 Euston Road
London
NW1 3BH

Franklin Watts Australia
Hachette Children's Books
Level 17/207 Kent Street
Sydney
NSW 2000

A CIP catalogue record for this book is available
from the British Library.

ISBN: 978 0 7496 7128 0 (hbk)
ISBN: 978 0 7496 7314 7 (pbk)

Series Editor: Jackie Hamley
Series Advisors: Dr Barrie Wade, Dr Hilary Minns
Series Designer: Peter Scoulding

Printed in China

Franklin Watts is a division of
Hachette Children's Books.

For Hayley, who might go for a run one day – P.K.

The Fun Run

by
Maggie Moore

Illustrated by
Peter Kavanagh

W
FRANKLIN WATTS
LONDON•SYDNEY

Maggie Moore
"I have been on a fun run, but I walked all the way. It was a fun walk for me!"

Peter Kavanagh
"I'm not very good at running, but I did win a famous race you might have heard of!"

Robin is ringing the bell
to kick off the Fun Run.

Will Quacking Duck win?

Fox is packing Duck
in a box.

Quacking Duck
cannot win.

Big Pig is puffing up the hill. Will Pig win?

Fox will lock Pig
in the shed.

Big Pig cannot win.

Quick Rat is rushing up the path. Will Rat win?

15

Fox will push Rat
in the bin.

Quick Rat cannot win.

Dog can jog up the hill,
but Dog cannot win.

Rabbit can hop, but
Rabbit cannot win.

Will Fox win?

21

Chick will win!

23

Notes for parents and teachers

READING CORNER PHONICS has been structured to provide maximum support for children learning to read through synthetic phonics. The stories are designed for independent reading but may also be used by adults for sharing with young children.

The teaching of early reading through synthetic phonics focuses on the 44 sounds in the English language, and how these sounds correspond to their written form in the 26 letters of the alphabet. Carefully controlled vocabulary makes these books accessible for children at different stages of phonics teaching, progressing from simple CVC (consonant-vowel-consonant) words such as "top" (t-o-p) to trisyllabic words such as "messenger" (mess-en-ger). READING CORNER PHONICS allows children to read words in context, and also provides visual clues and repetition to further support their reading. These books will help develop the all important confidence in the new reader, and encourage a love of reading that will last a lifetime!

If you are reading this book with a child, here are a few tips:

1. Talk about the story before you start reading. Look at the cover and the title. What might the story be about? Why might the child like it?

2. Encourage the child to reread the story, and to retell the story in their own words, using the illustrations to remind them what has happened.

3. Discuss the story and see if the child can relate it to their own experience, or perhaps compare it to another story they know.

4. Give praise! Small mistakes need not always be corrected. If a child is stuck on a word, ask them to try and sound it out and then blend it together again, or model this yourself. For example "wish" w-i-sh "wish".

READING CORNER PHONICS covers two grades of synthetic phonics teaching, with three levels at each grade. Each level has a certain number of words per story, indicated by the number of bars on the spine of the book:

GRADE 1	
50 words	CVC words with short vowel sounds
70 words	CVC words plus sounds of more than one letter
100 words	Sounds of more than one letter, simple polysyllabic words

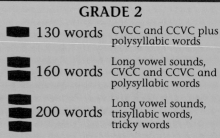

GRADE 2	
130 words	CVCC and CCVC plus polysyllabic words
160 words	Long vowel sounds, CVCC and CCVC and polysyllabic words
200 words	Long vowel sounds, trisyllabic words, tricky words